COMMISSION FOR SETTLING PRIVATE LAND CLAIMS IN CALIFORNIA.

TREATY STIPULATIONS BETWEEN MEXICO AND THE UNITED STATES.

ACT OF CONGRESS

OF MARCH 3, 1851.

INSTRUCTIONS

OF THE

DEPARTMENT OF THE INTERIOR

TO THE COMMISSIONERS.

REGULATIONS

OF THE COMMISSIONERS FOR THE PRESENTMENT AND PROSECUTION OF CLAIMS.

SAN FRANCISCO:
1852.

TREATY

BETWEEN

THE UNITED STATES AND MEXICO.

The Treaty of Guadalupe Hidalgo, concluded at that city on the 2nd day of February, 1848, between the United States of America and the United Mexican States, the ratifications of which were exchanged May 30, 1848, fixes a boundary line between the two governments, by which certain territory, including the present State of California, which had formerly belonged to Mexico, became the territory of the United States.

The Treaty then stipulates in Articles VIII. and IX. as follows, viz:

ARTICLE 8.—Mexicans now established in territories previously belonging to Mexico, and which remain for the future within the limits of the United States, as defined by the present treaty, shall be free to continue where they now reside, or to remove at any time to the Mexican republic, retaining the property which they possess in the said territories, or disposing thereof, and removing the proceeds wherever they please, without their being subjected, on this account, to any contribution, tax, or charge whatever.

Those who shall prefer to remain in the said territories, may either retain the title and rights of Mexican citizens, or acquire those of citizens of the United States. But they shall be under the obligation to make their elec-

ARTICULO 8.—Los Mexicanos establecídos hoy en territorios pertenecientes ántes á México, y que quedan para lo futuro dentro de los límites señalados por el presente tratado á los Estados Unidos, podrán permanecer en donde ahora habitan, ó trasladarse en cualquier tiempo á la república Mexicana, conservando en los indicados territorios los bienes que poseen, ó enagenandolos y pasando su valor á donde les convenga, sin que por esto pueda exigirseles ningun género de contribucion, gravámen ó impuesto.

Los que prefieran permanecer en los indicados territorios, podrán conservar el titulo y derechos de ciudadanos Mexicanos, ó adquirir el título y derechos de ciudadanos de los Estados Unidos. Mas la eleccion entra una y otra ciudada-

tion within one year from the date of the exchange of ratifications of this treaty; and those who shall remain in the said territories after the expiration of that year, without having declared their intention to retain the character of Mexicans, shall be considered to have elected to become citizens of the United States.

In the said territories, property of every kind, now belonging to Mexicans not established there, shall be inviolably respected.—The present owners, the heirs of these, and all Mexicans who may hereafter acquire said property by contract, shall enjoy with respect to it guaranties equally ample as if the same belonged to citizens of the United States.

nia deberan hacerla dentro de un año contado desde la fecha del cange de las ratificaciones de este tratado. Y los que permanecieren en los indicados territorios despues de transcurrido el año, sin haber declarado su intencion de retener el carácter de Mexicanos, se considerará que han elegido ser ciudadanos de los Estados Unidos.

Las propiedades de todo género existentes en los expresados territorios, y que pertenecen ahora á Mexicanos no establecidos en ellos, serán respetadas inviolablemente. Sus actuales dueños, los herederos de estos, y los Mexicanos que en lo venidero puedan adquirir por contrato las indicadas propiedades, disfrutarán respecto de ellas tan amplia garantia, como si perteneciesen á ciudadanos de los Estados Unidos.

Article 9.—The Mexicans who, in the territory aforesaid, shall not preserve the character of citizens of the Mexican republic, conformably with what is stipulated in the preceding article, shall be incorporated into the union of the United States and be admitted at the proper time (to be judged of by the Congress of the United States) to the enjoyment of all the rights of citizens of the United States, according to the principles of the Constitution; and in the mean time shall be maintained and protected in the free enjoyment of their liberty and property, and secured in the free exercise of their religion without restriction.

Articulo 9.—Los Mexicanos que, en los territorios antedichos, no conserven el carácter de ciudadanos de la republica Mexicana, segun lo estipulado en el artículo precedente serán incorporados en la union de los Estados Unidos, y se admitirán en tiempo oportuno (á juicio del Congreso de los Estados Unidos) al goce de todos los derechos de ciudadanos de los Estados Unidos conforme á los principios de la constitucion; y entretanto serán mantenidos y protegidos en el goce de su libertad y propiedad, y asegurados en el libre ejercicio de su religion sin restricion alguna.

AN ACT

TO ASCERTAIN AND SETTLE THE PRIVATE LAND CLAIMS IN THE STATE OF CALIFORNIA.

Be it enacted by the Senate and House of Representatives of the United States of America in Congress assembled, That for the purpose of ascertaining and settling private land claims in the State of California, a commission shall be, and is hereby, constituted, which shall consist of three Commissioners, to be appointed by the President of the United States, by and with the advice and consent of the Senate, which commission shall continue for three years from the date of this act, unless sooner discontinued by the President of the United States.

SEC. 2. *And be it further enacted,* That a secretary, skilled in the Spanish and English languages, shall be appointed by the said commissioners, whose duty it shall be to act as interpreter, and to keep a record of the proceedings of the board in a bound book, to be filed in the office of the Secretary of the Interior on the termination of the commission.

SEC. 3. *And be it further enacted,* That such clerks, not to exceed five in number, as may be necessary, shall be appointed by the said commissioners.

SEC. 4. *And be it further enacted,* That it shall be lawful for the President of the United States to appoint an agent learned in the law, and skilled in the Spanish and English languages, whose special duty it shall be to superintend the interests of the United States in the premises, to continue him in such agency as long as the public interest may, in the judgment of the President, require his continuance, and to allow him such compensation as the President shall deem reasonable. It shall be the duty of the said agent to attend the meetings of the

1*

board, to collect testimony in behalf of the United States, and to attend on all occasions when the claimant, in any case before the board, shall take depositions; and no deposition taken by or in behalf of any such claimant shall be read in evidence in any case, whether before the commissioners, or before the District or Supreme Court of the United States, unless notice of the time and place of taking the same shall have been given in writing to said agent, or to the District Attorney of the proper district, so long before the time of taking the deposition as to enable him to be present at the time and place of taking the same, and like notice shall be given of the time and place of taking any deposition on the part of the United States.

SEC. 5. *And be it further enacted*, That the said Commissioners shall hold their sessions at such times and places as the President of the United States shall direct, of which they shall give due and public notice; and the Marshal of the district in which the board is sitting shall appoint a deputy, whose duty it shall be to attend upon the said board, and who shall receive the same compensation as is allowed to the Marshal for his attendance upon the District Court.

SEC. 6. *And be it further enacted*, That the said commissioners, when sitting as a board, and each commissioner at his chambers, shall be, and are, and is hereby, authorised to administer oaths, and to examine witnesses in any case pending before the Commissioners, that all such testimony shall be taken in writing, and shall be recorded and preserved in bound books to be provided for that purpose.

SEC. 7. *And be it further enacted*, That the secretary of the board shall be, and he is hereby, authorized and required, on the application of the law agent or District Attorney of the United States, or of any claimant or his counsel, to issue writs of subpœna commanding the attendance of a witness or witnesses before the said board or any Commissioner.

SEC. 8. *And be it further enacted*, That each and every person claiming lands in California by virtue of any right or title derived from the Spanish or Mexican government, shall present the same to the said Commissioners when sitting as a board, together with such documentary evidence and testimony of witnesses as the said claimant relies upon in support of such claims; and it shall be the duty of the Commissioners, when the case is ready for hearing, to proceed promptly to examine the same upon such evidence, and upon the evidence produced in behalf of the United States, and to decide upon the validity of the said claim, and, within thirty days after such decision is rendered, to certify the same, with the reasons on which it is founded, to the District Attorney of the United States in and for the district in which such decision shall be rendered.

SEC. 9. *And be it further enacted*, That in all cases of the rejection or confirmation of any claim by the board of Commissioners, it shall and may be lawful for the claimant or the District Attorney, in behalf of the United States, to present a petition to the District Court of the district in which the land claimed is situated, praying the said court to review the decision of the said Commissioners, and to decide on the validity of such claim; and such petition, if presented by the claimant, shall set forth fully the nature of the claim and the names of the original and present claimants, and shall contain a deraignment of the claimant's title, together with a transcript of the report of the board of Commissioners, and of the documentary evidence and testimony of the witnesses on which it was founded; and such petition, if presented by the District Attorney in behalf of the United States, shall be accompanied by a transcript of the report of the board of Commissioners, and of the papers and evidence on which it was founded, and shall fully and distinctly set forth the grounds on which the said claim is alleged to be invalid, a copy of which petition, if the same shall be presented by a claimant, shall be served on the District Attorney of the United States, and, if presented in behalf of the United States, shall be served on the claimant or his attorney; and the party upon whom such service shall be made shall be bound to answer the same within a time to be prescribed by the judge of the District Court; and the answer of the claimant to such petition shall set forth fully the nature of the claim, and the names of the original and present claimants, and shall contain a deraignment of the claimant's title; and the answer of the District Attorney in behalf of the United States shall fully and distinctly set forth the grounds on which the said claim is alleged to be invalid, copies of which answers shall be served upon the adverse party thirty days before the meeting of the court, and thereupon, at the first term of the court thereafter, the said case shall stand for trial, unless, on cause shown, the same shall be continued by the court.

Sec. 10. *And be it further enacted*, That the District Court shall proceed to render judgment upon the pleadings and evidence in the case, and upon such further evidence as may be taken by order of the said court, and shall, on application of the party against whom judgment is rendered, grant an appeal to the Supreme Court of the United States, on such security for costs in the District and Supreme Court, in case the judgment of the District Court shall be affirmed, as the said court shall prescribe; and if the court shall be satisfied that the party desiring to appeal is unable to give such security, the appeal may be allowed without security.

Sec. 11. *And be it further enacted*, That the Commissioners herein provided for, and the District and Supreme Courts, in deciding on the validity of any claim brought before them under the provisions of this act, shall be governed by the treaty of Guadalupe Hidalgo, the law of nations, the laws, usages, and customs of the government from which the claim is derived, the principles of equity, and the decisions of the Supreme Court of the United States, so far as they are applicable.

Sec. 12. *And be it further enacted*, That to entitle either party to a review of the proceedings and decision of the Commissioners hereinbefore provided for, notice of the intention of such party to file a petition to the District Court shall be entered on the journal or record of proceedings of the Commissioners within sixty days after their decision on the claim has been made and notified to the parties, and such petition shall be filed in the District Court within six months after such decison has been rendered.

Sec. 13. *And be it further enacted*, That all lands, the claims to which have been finally rejected by the Commissioners in manner herein provided, or which shall be finally decided to be invalid by the District or Supreme Court, and all lands the claims to which shall not have been presented to the said Commissioners within two years after the date of this act, shall be deemed, held, and considered as part of the public domain of the United States; and for all claims finally confirmed by the said Commissioners, or by the said District or Supreme Court, a patent shall issue to the claimant upon his presenting to the General Land Office an authentic certificate of such confirmation, and a plat or survey of the said land, duly certified and approved by the Surveyor-General of California, whose duty it shall be to cause all private claims which shall be finally confirmed to be accurately surveyed, and to furnish plats of the same; and in the location of the said claims, the said Surveyor-General shall have the same power and authority as are conferred on the register of the land office and receiver of the public moneys of Louisiana, by the sixth section of the act "to create the office of surveyor of the public lands for the State of Louisiana," approved third March, one thousand eight hundred and thirty-one: *Provided, always*, That if the title of the claimant to such lands shall be contested by any other person, it shall and may be lawful for such person to present a petition to the District Judge of the United States for the district in which the lands are situated, plainly and distinctly setting forth his title thereto, and praying the said judge to hear and determine the same, a copy of which petition shall be served upon the adverse party thirty days before the time appointed for hearing the same. *And provided, further*, That it shall and may be lawful for the District Judge of the United States, upon the hearing of such petition, to grant an injunction to restrain the party at whose instance the claim to the said lands has been confirmed, from suing out a patent for the same, until the title thereto shall have been finally decided, a copy of which order shall be transmitted to the Commissioner of the General Land Office, and thereupon no patent shall issue until such decision shall be made, or until sufficient time shall, in the opinion of the said Judge, have been allowed for obtaining the same; and thereafter the said injunction shall be dissolved.

Sec. 14. *And be it further enacted*, That the provisions of this act shall not extend to any town lot, farm lot, or pasture lot, held under a grant from any corporation or town to which lands may have been granted for the establishment of a town by the Spanish or Mexican government, or the lawful authorities thereof, nor to any city, or town, or village lot, which city, town, or village existed on the seventh day of July, eighteen hundred and forty-six; but the claim for the same shall be presented by the corporate authorities of the said town, or where the land on which the said city, town, or village was originally granted to an individual, the claim shall be presented by or in the name of such individual, and the fact of the existence of the said city, town, or village on the said seventh July, eighteen hundred and forty-six, being duly proved, shall be prima facie evidence of a grant to such corporation, or to the individual under whom the said lot-holders claim; and where any city, town, or village shall be in existence at the time of passing this act, the claim for the land embraced within the limits of the same may be made by the corporate authority of the said city, town or village.

Sec. 15. *And be it further enacted*, That the final decrees rendered by the said Commissioners, or by the District or Supreme Court of the United States, or any patent to be issued under this act, shall be conclusive between the United States and the said claimants only, and shall not affect the interests of third persons.

Sec. 16. *And be it further enacted*, That it shall be the duty of the Commissioners herein provided for to ascertain and report to the Secretary of the Interior the tenure by which the mission lands are held, and those held by civilized Indians, and those who are engaged in agriculture or labor of any kind, and also those which are occupied and cultivated by Pueblos or Rancheros Indians.

Sec. 17. *And be it further enacted*, That each Commissioner appointed under this act shall be allowed and paid at the rate of six thousand dollars per annum; that the secretary of the Commissioners shall be allowed and paid at the rate of four thousand dollars per annum; and the clerks herein provided for shall be allowed and paid at the rate of one thousand five hundred dollars per annum; the aforesaid salaries to commence from the day of the notification by the Commissioners of the first meeting of the board.

Sec. 18. *And be it further enacted*, That the secretary of the board shall receive no fee except for furnishing certified copies of any paper or record, and for issuing writs of subpœna. For furnishing certified copies of any paper or record, he shall receive twenty cents for every hundred words, and for issuing writs of subpœna, fifty cents for each witness; which fees shall be equally divided between the said secretary and the assistant clerk.

Approved, March 3, 1851.

INSTRUCTIONS TO THE COMMISSSIONERS

FROM THE

DEPARTMENT OF THE INTERIOR.

GENERAL LAND OFFICE,
September 11*th*, 1851.

GENTLEMEN:—You have been appointed Commissioners to discharge the important and responsible duties prescribed by Act of Congress, approved 3d March, 1851, entitled "An Act to ascertain and settle the private Land Claims in the State of California," which authorizes the continuance of the Commission for three years from the date of the law, unless sooner terminated by the President of the United States.

The act charges you with the appointment of a Secretary "skilled in the Spanish and English languages, to act as interpreter, and to keep a record of the proceedings of the Board, in a bound book, to be filed in the office of the Secretary of the Interior, on the termination of the Commission," and provides for the employment, by you, not to exceed five, of such a number of Clerks "as may be necessary."

It further authorizes the appointment, by the President, which will be duly made, of a Law Agent, skilled in both the languages mentioned, "whose special duty it shall be to superintend the interests of the United States in the premises."

This law has made ample provision for the accomplishment of the great object of the Government, which is, to ascertain, settle, and recognize all *bona fide* valid titles derived from the former sovereignties of the country, and to detect and forever put at rest all fabricated, fraudulent, or simulated grants.

The growth and prosperity of California materially depends upon a speedy and just settlement of the claims to lands within her limits, and the separation of all private property from the public domain, so that the public lands in that State may be disposed of as Congress may hereafter direct, without danger of conflict in title, or interference with the rights of individuals.

You are therefore directed to proceed at once to San Francisco, in California.

Immediately upon your arrival, you will hold your first sessions at that place, agreeably to the order of the President, giving due and public notice of the fact, as required by law.

You will give timely advice to the Department, of such other places as you would recommend that your subsequent sessions should be held.

The 8th Section of the said Act of the 3d March, 1851, declares as follows:

"That each and every person claiming lands in California, by virtue of any right or title, derived from the Spanish or Mexican Governments, shall present the same to the said Commissioners, when sitting as a Board, together with such documentary evidence and testimony of witnesses as the said claimant relies upon in support of such claims; and it shall be the duty of the Commissioners, when the case is ready for hearing, to proceed promptly to examine the same upon such evidence, and upon the evidence produced in behalf of the United States, and decide upon the validity of the said claim, and within thirty days after such decision is rendered, to certify the same with the reasons on which it is founded, to the District Attorney of the United States, in and for the District in which such decision shall be rendered."

This, in connection with the 14th Section, which relates to property under *Corporate Grants*, shows the classes of titles in which the claimants have authority for bringing their claims before the Commissioners for adjudication, and in which, after obtaining a decision, both the Claimants and the United States have a right, on petition, to have such decision reviewed by the United States Courts, with a right of appeal to the Supreme Court of the United States.

The 11th Section of the Act points to the *data* which shall control in the adjudications, by directing as follows:

"That the Commissioners herein provided for, and the District and Supreme Courts, in deciding on the validity of any claim brought before them, under the provisions of this act, shall be governed by the Treaty of Guadalupe Hidalgo, the law of Nations, the laws, usages and customs of the Government from which the claim is derived, the principles of Equity, and the decisions of the Supreme Court of the United States, so far as they are applicable."

The Treaty of Guadalupe Hidalgo, concluded at that city, on the 2d February, 1848, the ratifications of which were exchanged on the 30th May, 1848, expressly stipulates in the 8th and 9th articles, for the security and protection of the property of individuals, and in this respect not only employs, in substance, the language that is used in the Treaty of 1803, by which the former province of Louisiana was ceded to the United States by the French Republic; but conforms to the universally acknowledged principles of the laws of nations, which interdict interference to the prejudice of private property, upon a change of Sovereignty.

By the Act of Congress, approved 26th May, 1824, (United States Statutes at large, volume 4, page 52, chapter 173,) entitled "An Act enabling the claimants to lands within the limits of the State of Missouri, and Territory of Arkansas, to institute proceedings to try the validity of their claims," the Courts were opened for the adjudication of any title of a certain class in Missouri and Arkansas, which was claimed to be protected or secured by the Treaty of 1803, with the French Republic, and which might have been perfected into a complete title, under and in conformity to the laws, usages and customs of the Government under which the same originated, had not the Sovereignty of the country been transferred to the United States.

The Act of 1824, with certain modifications, was extended to Florida by the Act of Congress, approved 23d of May, 1828, entitled "An Act supplementary to the several Acts, providing for the settlement and confirmation of private land claims in Florida,"—U. S. Statutes at large, vol. 4, page 284, chap. 70.

Numerous cases, on appeal, under these laws, and other cases on writs of error, in which actions in the Courts below had been instituted in the nature of ejectments, have been brought before the Supreme Court of the United States, where the rights of property under inchoate titles derived from the Spanish authori-

2

ties have been examined, the principles of the laws of nations and the principles of equity under our own legislation have been asserted, expounded and applied to the species of property in question, and the whole subject most elaborately and ably discussed by that high tribunal, the most of the decisions of which, in land causes, will be found in Peters' and Howard's Reports of the decisions of the Supreme Court of the United States.

Besides the Treaty of 1848 with Mexico, as found in the 9th volume of the United States Statutes at large, the law of nations and the principles of equity as contained in works of authority from which your own judgment will enable you to make a proper selection, and the aforesaid decisions of the Supreme Court, in Peters' and Howard's Reports, in which the principles of public law and of equity are developed, the aforesaid 11th section of the Act of 3d March, 1851, requires that in adjudicating, you shall be governed by the laws, usages, and customs of the government from which the claim is derived.

There are claims in California derived from the authorities of old Spain, as well as from Mexico, and it will therefore be necessary to refer to, and consult the laws of Spain, the Royal Ordinances, the Decrees, and Regulations, which may be found in White's New Recopilacion in two volumes, relative to the disposal of the Royal Domain, in order to form a just idea of the policy and general principles which obtained and controlled in her land system.

I refer you also to the Report dated March 1st, 1849, of the Secretary of State for the Territory of California.

1st. " On the laws and regulations governing grants or sales of Public Lands in California," not only during the government of old Spain, but subsequently during the continuance of the Mexican power, and up to the period when the United States succeeded to the sovereignty.

2nd. " On the laws and regulations respecting the lands and other property belonging to the Missions of California."

3d. " On the titles of land in California, which may be required for fortifications, arsenals, or other military structures, for the use of the General Government of the United States."

This Report, with the accompanying Appendix, 1 to 33, is printed in Ex. Doc. No. 17, House of Representatives, 1st Sess., 31st Congress, pages 119 to 182 inclusive.

You are requested to obtain for the use of the Commission, authentic copies, in the *original* of the Laws, Regulations, etc., which are referred to in said Report. Also, a copy of the work therein mentioned entitled "Ordinanzas de Tierras y Aguas" by "Marianas Galuan, Edition of 1844," with such other official documents or papers as may have a material and useful bearing upon the matters which are to engage your attention in the duties devolved upon you by law,—all of which and of such other books as you may require, you will have properly bound, and labelled with the name of the "COMMISSION" and as the "*Property of the United States.*"

You will find in Senate Report, Com. No. 75, 1st Session, 30th Congress, testimony taken before a Committee of the Senate touching grants in California illegally made, and without the usual formalities, to which I would invite your careful consideration. The United States Surveyor General for California, whose office is at San Francisco, has obtained possession of the archives of the former Sovereignties of California, and has engaged a competent person to arrange, classify and index them, in such a manner as to be available in the examination of titles. This work of arrangement, if not already finished, will be completed by the time you will be able to reach the country.

The Surveyor General will be instructed to lay open to you those archives during your session at San Francisco, and to have prepared either a complete synopsis, or summary of the contents of each of the archives, or fac simile copies of the whole, whichever you may prefer, so as to be in readiness for delivery to you when you shall find it necessary to leave that place to visit other points.

With such materials to guide the Commission, you will enter upon the business of adjudication. You will require the claimant in every case, to file a written *notice* setting forth the name of "Present Claimant"—name of "Original Claimant"—nature of claim—its date—from whom the original title was derived—with a reference to the evidence of the power and authority under which the granting officer may have acted—quantity claimed—locality—nature and extent of conflicting claim, if any—with a reference to the documentary evidence and testimony relied upon to establish the claim, and to show a transfer of right from the "Original Grantee" to "Present Claimant."

You will also require the claimant, in all cases, to file a duly authenticated plat of survey, exhibiting the tract claimed, and showing the nature and extent of any claim interfering therewith.

This is deemed indispensable, in order by such initiatory survey to fix with precision and certainty the limits of every tract claimed, thereby avoiding, in regard to location, all doubt or controversy hereafter, in case of confirmation, and furnishing, at the same time, to the Commission, and to the Courts, evidence of the existence and nature of conflicting claims.

There are, it is believed, no Spanish or Mexican plats of Survey extant of lands in California; no actual surveys, so far as this office is advised, having ever been executed during the sovereignty over the countries of either Spain or Mexico.

The surveys, therefore, of all claims which may be brought before the Commissioners should be required to be executed, *at the expense of the parties*, in accordance with such orders, as you may deem necessary and proper in each case, and to be made under the superintendance of the United States Surveyor General, by whom the surveys, and any interference which may exist, should be examined and certified.

The effect of this will be, not only to save claimants from embarrassments and difficulties, inseparable from the presentation and adjudication of claims with indefinite limits, but it will promote the welfare of the country generally, by furnishing the Surveyor General with evidence of what is claimed as private property, thus enabling him to ascertain what is undisputed public land, and to proceed with the public surveys accordingly, without awaiting the final action of the different tribunals upon private titles.

The papers, in every case, should be regularly numbered, and entered in the order of presentation, in a *Docket* of the form herewith.

Your *Journal*, to consist of a substantially bound volume, or volumes, and prefaced by a record of your commissions, and oaths of office, should contain a full record of the notice, and evidence in support of each claim, and of your decision, setting forth, as succinctly and concisely as possible, all the leading facts, particulars, and the principles applicable to the case, and upon which such decision may be founded.

As a case may be acted upon by you at different periods, before being finally decided, the connexion of your proceedings may be kept up by page-references both in the Journal, and with the Docket. All the original papers should, of course, be carefully numbered, filed, and preserved, and should have an endorsement upon each of them of the volume and page of the record, in which they may be entered.

The 8th section of the Act, as herein before indicated, requires you "within thirty days after such decision is rendered, to certify the same, with the reasons on which it is founded, to the District Attorney of the United States in and for the District in which such decision shall be rendered."

This requirement will, of course, be strictly and uniformly observed by you, and the necessary entries of your action in the premises made on your record.

It will be observed that the 12th section of the act declares "that to entitle either party to a review of the proceedings and decision of the Commissioners, notice of the intention of such party to file a petition to the District Court shall be entered on the *Journal*, or record of proceedings of the Commissioners, within sixty days after their decision on the claim has been made and notified to the parties, and such petition shall be filed in the District Court within six months after such decision has been rendered."

This provision of law renders it necessary that you shall regularly notify the claimants, also, of your decision—and this should always be done promptly, and in any case in which the requisite notice of the intention to file a petition in Court shall not be given to you within sixty days from the time you may notify the parties of your decision, such decision will, *ipso facto*, become final and conclusive, and you will of course report any such case to the Surveyor General and to the Department.

It is a matter of high public concern, and of the deepest interest to California, that the business of the Commission should be pressed forward with all convenient dispatch, and as much so as is compatible with the grave interests involved, and when your labors, in regard to the classes of titles contemplated in the foregoing shall have terminated, you will give due notice of the fact to this office, and will turn over the records and papers to the Surveyor General, subject to the orders of the Department. Besides the duties hereinbefore adverted to, the Act of

3d March, 1851, requires, in its 16th section, that "the Commissioners shall ascertain and report to the Secretary of the Interior, the tenure by which the Mission Lands are held, and those held by civilized Indians, and those who are engaged in agriculture, or labor of any kind, and also those which are occupied or cultivated by Pueblos and Rancheros Indians."

You are directed to make a separate and full report on the several subjects specified in this section of the act, at as early a period as may be consistent with your other duties, under the law.

Your salaries, as stipulated in the 17th section of the act, will "commence from the day of the notification," by you, "of the first meeting of the Board."

Very respectfully,

Your obedient servant,

[Signed] J. BUTTERFIELD,

Commissioner.

Messrs. HILAND HALL, HARRY I. THORNTON and JAMES WILSON, United States Commissioners for the adjudication of California Land Claims.

The foregoing instructions are approved.

[Signed] ALEX. H. H. STUART,

Secretary.

DEPARTMENT OF THE INTERIOR, Sept. 11th, 1851.

REGULATIONS OF THE COMMISSIONERS.

The mode of bringing the claims specified in the Act of March 3, 1851, before the Commissioners, shall be by petition in writing, signed by the claimant or his counsel, addressed to the Commissioners, and filed with the Secretary of the Board, which petition shall set forth the names of the original and present claimants; the nature of the claim; the dates of the original grant and of the several assignments or conveyances, with the names of the parties thereto, through which the present claimant deduces his title; from whom the original title was derived; the power or authority under which the granting officer acted; the quantity of land claimed; its locality; when surveyed and when certified by the Surveyor General, (if thus surveyed and certified;) and the nature and extent of every known interfering claim; with a reference to the documentary and other evidence relied upon by the claimant; and said petition shall be accompanied by a copy of the original grant and a translation of the same, or by reasons for not furnishing them.

If the claimant desires to prosecute his claim in person, he will, on application for that purpose, be aided by a Clerk of the Board in the preparation of his petition, without charge; and will be allowed all proper facilities in the prosecution of his claim.

The Commissioners as a board, or at their several chambers, will attend to the taking of testimony in behalf of the claimants or of the United States, in cases which are prepared therefor, on due notice being given to the Law Agent or the claimant, as required by law.

The Commissioners will from time to time, as occasion may require, adopt and make known such further rules and regulations as shall seem best calculated to facilitate the prosecution of the business before them, and to bring it to a speedy and satisfactory termination.

The Commissioners will be in session for the reception of claims and the transaction of business on the twenty-first day of January, instant, and until otherwise ordered.

Office of the Commissioners,
San Francisco, January 10th, 1852.

By order of the Board:

J. B. CARR, *Secretary*.

www.ingramcontent.com/pod-product-compliance
Lightning Source LLC
LaVergne TN
LVHW020636110826
845149LV00004B/1229
9781418191191